PRAISE FOR
Stop Letting Your Customers Down

"Finally, a book that speaks to today's online marketers, written by a decades-long expert in the field. I've had the pleasure of working with Brett across multiple companies and have seen him develop his impressive skills first hand. I'd highly recommend *Stop Letting Your Customers Down*."

—CHRIS FRALIC, PARTNER FIRST ROUND CAPITAL

"Bair talks about today's online customers and the ways in which marketers can optimize each and every connection."

—ANTHONY BUCCI, CO-FOUNDER REVZILLA

About

Stop Letting Your Customers Down

For decades, online marketers have been waiting for technology to catch up to their needs and visions. As odd as it sounds in our incredibly tech-savvy and tech-saturated world, marketers have long known that more could be done to reach customers and to improve their online experiences. Businesses big and small could grow infinitely—if only...

Now, of course, everyone and their grandmother has heard about Big Data. Now, marketers have access not only to the broad and more precise data they need, but also to the tools that will make that data useful. Most importantly, marketers now can improve upon the customer experience in ways and at speeds that did not exist just a few years ago. Making changes at the macro and micro level, modern-day marketers can make the online experience feel truly unique across multiple demographics and devices.

Gone forever is the idea of a one-size-fits-all mentality for online customers—today, if your business is not focused on creating a customer-centric experience, your business is in peril. If your numbers look good, but you are not utilizing the marketing tools available to you, you are already far behind. Today's ever-connected customer is more educated and powerful than ever and it is up to marketers to stay agile and deliver in ways they previously have not. *Stop Letting Your Customers Down: How to Build a Better Digital Experience* was written with a sharp ear to what customers are telling businesses via their keystrokes. Online marketers and businesses will want to embrace the insights and challenges this book presents, in order to stay relevant, necessary, and competitive.

STOP
Letting Your Customers Down

How to Build a Better
Digital Experience

BRETT BAIR

Copyright © 2015 by Brett Bair

For more information contact:
Monetate
951 E. Hector Street
Conshohocken, PA 19428 USA

978-0-692-39795-4 Paperback
978-0-692-39794-7 eBook

Library of Congress Control Number: 2015903352

CONTENTS

CHAPTER 1

Why Your Marketing Isn't Getting Results Fast Enough

I have always been impressed by great suit salesmen who are able to know your size from halfway across the room. The best simply say, "The 42 longs are right over there." The salesman immediately creates the illusion that they know who I am and convey a level of expertise that will make my experience very successful. This personalized approach has another great effect. Because I now feel like I am working with a trusted advisor, the salesperson can easily upsell a tie, shirt, or even a new pair of shoes to complete the entire look. And guess what—during this process I am typically less concerned over price because the entire experience was worth it.

Back in the days of old-school marketing—just five years ago—most companies were still relying on the traditional marketing practice of throwing more money at their online advertising campaigns and celebrating a 2-percent conversion rate. When your company is pulling in millions, converting 2 percent could be considered a decent enough achievement, but is it really? If 98 percent of the people coming to your site aren't converting, how can you celebrate? Where are all your potential customers going if they aren't converting? Don't be complacent. Don't think that changes you made five years ago are still having enough of an effect today.

If you want to move ahead of your competitors, begin by assuming they aren't conducting business the way they were five years ago. If you want to push forward, I ask you to first take a step back and look at how you are managing your business. If you are still working from a basic traffic-and-conversion mindset and sense that there is much more to the equation—read on. If you have moved past that old mindset and have already begun to look deeper into your data and deeper at your customer base—congratulations—but my bet is that there is still much more you can do.

Heck, just five years ago, companies big and small were still facing the challenge of creating an online experience that reflected an in-store experience. Technology moves so fast, it's easy to forget how much more pleasant and simplified our online shopping experiences have become—much like we already forget what our old Facebook page and news feed looked like. And MySpace—wasn't that all just a flashing hot pink or neon green font ticking across a black background?

Five years ago, companies did have the technology to create more impressive and effective online customer experiences, but it was often expensive and hard to use. Marketing teams had plenty of ideas, but tech teams were busy focusing on larger backend tech issues rather than what they considered small-time perpetual needs of customers and potential customers. Higher-ups might monitor their company's website on a weekly basis and be content with nuanced changes as long as profit margins remained robust, but they really never knew if consumers noticed those nuanced changes—changes that had cost so much money to develop, test, and create.

For decades, the traditional marketing model in which the product was at the center of the hub and the customer was one spoke of the wheel—along with a brick-and-mortar store, catalog, and website—has ruled. Everything about the business revolved around pushing the product. Yes, businesses talked about the customer and the ubiquitous "The customer is always right" slogan emerged, but only in very recent history—thanks to sweeping technological and cultural changes—has the customer actually moved to the center of the marketing model. For most successful businesses now, the customer is at the hub of the wheel with the brick-and-mortar store, catalog, website, Facebook, Instagram, Pinterest, Snapchat, Yelp, Flickr, FourSquare, and Twitter revolving around him or her nonstop.

Just staying on top of which social media platforms are most popular and most relevant today can feel like a 24/7 job. Consider just a few of the selected statistics below and how by the time you hold this book in your hands, these numbers will more than likely already be outdated:

- In 2013, the 45–54 year age bracket was the fastest growing demographic on Facebook. The fastest growing bracket on Twitter was even older (*Buffer*, July 16, 2013).
- Seventy-three percent of US Internet users who use Facebook make over $75,000 annually, compared to 17 percent of Twitter users (*Business Insider*, October 18, 2013).

- In the 2012 *Huffington Post* article "100 Fascinating Social Media Statistics and Figures From 2012"—which went viral and was instantly translated into an infographic by iStrategyLabs—80 percent of Internet users preferred to "connect with brands on Facebook," and time spent on Instagram exceeded time spent on Twitter—for the very first time.

These studies analyze, as we know, which demographic is on which site at what hour of the day and on what device—all crucial data for marketers. But even when we set specific numbers and media aside, an overall sense that marketers are in a frenzy to catch up and keep up prevails. In a study conducted in 2013 ("Digital Distress: What Keeps Marketers Up at Night?"[1]) over three-quarters of the 1,000 marketers polled stated that they think "marketing has changed more in the past two years than in the past fifty." Furthermore, although roughly fifty percent of respondents reported they believed their "digital marketing efforts were working," less than ten percent checked "strongly agree" in this metric. Finally, when asked to state their top concerns

1 Adobe

in their own words, marketers noted the need not to simply keep up with the pace of digital marketing, but to stay ahead of the curve.

Speed and timing today mean more to marketers than they ever have. The attention span of your visitors and customers is waning. You have, in many cases, not minutes but fractions of a second to grab their attention. Getting the right message in front of the right customer at the right time is a critical part of establishing a positive relationship. Customers are becoming more and more aware of the amount of data they are sharing with you, and it is up to you to take that data in the moment and give the customer the content, product, offer, and information that makes sense and keeps them coming back for more.

Culling some of the more dismaying revelations from the studies above is not meant to drive professionals who already feel less than proficient in digital marketing over the edge. On the contrary—the research is a call to marketers to be bold and trained in all matters digital. It is a call for CEOs and company leaders to set aside a percentage of their departmental budget for experimentation. Having worked in online commerce since its earliest days, I feel it is my duty to sound the alarm to those who are still conducting business as usual: "But our numbers are strong, why change?" The truth is, even if you are currently tripping over profits, that can only last so long. In fact, some of the largest most successful businesses may be the furthest out of touch with what it is that customers want. Customer expectations are evolving at warp speed, and companies that put off their ability to meet those expectations, even for one day, will undoubtedly be left in the dust.

At the risk of sounding like a broken record, just five years ago—okay, maybe ten—it took a lot to bring a business down. A pharmaceutical company that was once a household name might have one of its over-the-counter products removed from the shelves (and never trusted again), if its product had been tampered with and had resulted in a number of deaths. Nowadays, it takes one dissatisfied customer with a Twitter account to ruin sales—or destroy a brand name. One person complaining to just one hundred followers may result not in death by a thousand cuts, but death in hundreds of thousands of shared 140-character tweets.

Customers are moving incredibly fast, and so is their word. Word of mouth does not mean what it used to—#hatethatcompany has power and travels at the speed of light. Luckily, #love is one of the top five hashtags on Instagram—or at least it was in 2012—but again, companies cannot risk losing even one "like" in this era of digital consumerism. Partnering with Monetate means moving just as fast as your customers or faster. It means developing a conversation with each and every customer in order to provide a memorable, meaningful, and compelling experience that leaves them wanting to buy more from you—and very possibly tweeting and spreading the word that others should #loveyou and buy from you too.

When a nightmare situation does arise—say your company is suddenly alerted that its online checkout process is not functioning—you need to have tools that help you to quickly inform customers of the problem, and to provide other purchasing options. Not long ago, such a crisis would have entailed the IT department working double-duty—solving the glitch and rolling out site changes to inform customers of the issue. In the time it took the development team to sort through everything, hundreds or thousands of customers may have turned elsewhere to do business.

If personalization tools remained burdensome and technical problems time consuming, you can imagine the number of overtime hours people tallied when they needed to make a timely, sales-boosting change to their company's website. When I worked at CDNow, we faced this challenge any time a popular music artist passed away or was suddenly popping up in the news. The sooner we could change our home page to highlight a deceased or newsworthy musician, the better, but in 1998, it took a team of designers, merchandisers, developers, and marketers to stop everything and work all day and night to make the changes that would make it easier for customers to access the featured artist.

Fast forward to 2014, a single person could leverage a tool like Monetate—creating a new home page experience and having it out in the real world in a matter of minutes, as soon as he or she saw fit. The future people imagined might come one day is here. The game of doing online business has changed, and only those who have been standing at the ready—excited to embrace the new rules and tools—have been able to run straight out of the starting blocks into the new territory full speed. Only those who expected the future of online commerce to come as soon as it has have found themselves able to adapt quickly and produce impressive results.

I have seen clients respond with brilliant, if not sometimes tongue-in-cheek marketing campaigns, in a moment's notice. A few years ago, when a rare earthquake hit New York City, clothing designer Marc Eckō offered a special sale to those in the affected area.

When winter snowstorms crushed the East Coast, The Container Store ran campaigns to encourage customers who couldn't get out to order online. Similarly, Godiva warned its customers in advance that some Valentine's Day orders would not make the expected delivery dates due to extreme inclement weather. The point is, even when customers are going to be disappointed, alerting them to the fact shows a level of customer care that will be appreciated and remembered. It is always crucial to go the extra mile for your customers and to stay one step ahead of your customers and your competitors.

Online businesses are growing in number and are becoming more competitive, thanks in part to the evolution of open source technology, cloud-based hosting solutions, and business-user oriented tools. E-commerce is nothing like it once was—look at what Kickstarter is doing for the product-manufacturing world and people in the creative arts. Many older businesses are being held back by outdated expensive infrastructures and technology investments. Lightening the load and honing in on what counts now more than ever—that customer—is crucial to remaining in the game.

Our clients' wish lists might include getting help on everything from website testing, email optimization, and personalization to behavioral, contextual, and situational targeting. One thing all our clients want is to improve their entire online purchasing process. By taking a thorough look at their specific needs, we are able to offer tailored solutions.

Clients who once had to communicate with several different teams while trying out only one or two test campaigns at a time can now run multiple campaigns simultaneously and shave hours off of interdepartmental meetings by simply pulling up and sharing data. Businesses who partner with us are able to launch new campaigns within days not weeks. Our clients report that they are learning more about what resonates with their customers—new and returning—more quickly and more in-depth. Clients tell us they are now confident they can pinpoint the spikes they see in online sales to specific changes they have made rather than to random factors.

In 2014, Monetate influenced one in every three dollars spent online during "Cyber Week"—the holiday shopping season comprising Black Friday through Cyber Monday. In December 2014 alone Monetate delivered 12 billion personalized experiences. In 2013, our partner Famous Footwear was awarded a Gold Medal in the Channel Innovation Awards—which go to retailers, big and small, who are "using new technologies and innovative strategies to satisfy customers." In the next year and into the future, Monetate is determined to continue turning all its creative and technological energies toward the realization of better and more powerful customer experience tools.

Big name brands that take the leap and set customer experience optimization as a top priority show amazing results—fast. It is true that the concept of website optimization has been around for some time now, but it is the implementation and practice of customer experience optimization that sets the most successful businesses apart. I first learned to understand online customers in the nineties, and more than two decades later, I know that when today's smart and fast-moving customer comes to a website, they expect more than novelty.

That is to say, novelty that doesn't make the experience more useful and relevant to the customer can quickly come to feel nothing short of gimmicky. Greeting a customer by his or her first name has become standard e-commerce practice and mentioning the weather conditions in your customer's area and offering up Live Chat assistance is helpful too—but what ultimately matters, what has always ultimately mattered, is that the customer leaves the experience not feeling like he or she is part of one singular body your business has labeled "customer."

Prior to joining Monetate, I worked for several new business startups and top e-commerce firms. I was the product category manager of music, movies, and video games for Half.com when eBay decided to buy us in 2000. It was exciting to be part of a company that was not only the first used product retailer to get products listed on comparison shopping sites, but to be part of the team that developed the process of integrating existing digital images and liner notes for a product with its bar code—something eBay had yet to do. It was a thrill to immediately get eBay's attention, which in 2000 was already a leader in online commerce and a household name; but it was more of a thrill to watch them then hit the ball out of the park and be able to offer a vastly improved customer experience—for example, by offering the Buy It Now option—after they acquired Half. Buy It Now is now the norm on Ebay instead of Auctions.

Everything I have brought to Monetate from my previous positions is geared directly toward improving the customer experience. Being part of the booming e-commerce field in its earliest days felt cutting edge, but it was frustrating too. When I began to realize where the online customer experience could and should go, but saw where it got stalled because of the limits of tools and technology, I strengthened my resolve to seek out a company that was working on products I would personally want to buy, use, and promote. Years of watching too many businesses leave too many potentially excellent opportunities by the wayside motivated me to seek out a team of innovative marketing professionals that were merging creativity and technology in the most agile of ways. Becoming part of the Monetate team has allowed me to open the eyes of hundreds of clients by offering them tools that maximize their online capability, agility, and presence.

You want tools that focus not on vanity, but on utility—from relevant product discovery, to effective upsells and cross-sells, to the final stage of a no-brainer checkout. Today's multitasking online customer can be slowed down. If you engage them, you can bring them loyally back time and time again. By integrating demographic data with behavioral data, you will begin to know your customers so well that their shopping experience feels seamlessly unique to them—and actually is.

East Coast, West Coast? That's easy. Affluent area or rural—easy too. A blizzard or a hurricane coming in—thank you, Weather Channel. But knowing better how each customer shops and what they actually do—do they fill a cart and leave it, do they wait for special offers, are they on an everything-in-purple binge—will help your business to adapt on multiple levels.

Today's consumer is more of an open book than ever, and not just in terms of marketing data, but in terms of the personal information he or she is willing to share. We aren't just talking about how you finally convinced your grandparents that it is now safe to shop online—we are talking about social media, selfies, real customers posing in your clothing or using your gear and posting it to your website—the list is infinite, as is your company's potential in moving its marketing efforts forward.

This type of technological evolution won't end. A full 90 percent of all the data in the world has been generated over the last two years.[2] Today's data is stored in terabytes (trillions) and petabytes (quadrillions), but by 2020, experts predict that up to 35 zettabytes (sextillions) of data will be created annually.[3]

The numbers are so outrageous, they are almost impossible to identify with—but the main takeaway is that the gap between customer expectations and a

2 SINTEF
3 International Data Corporation (IDC)

company's ability to deliver is already widening as data figures explode. Companies that jump on the data do deliver. Clorox credited its 2013 increase in sales to data mining social media for flu trends, and using that data to determine where to stock its products. Walmart does over 1 million in-store transactions per hour—combine that POS data with that of social media and e-commerce, and you have multiple data resources to mine on each and every customer.[4]

Clorox and Walmart are just two examples of major players finding new ways to compete. Once you shed the one-size-fits-all mentality, you will become more agile than your competitors. When you know exactly what sells, when and why it sells, and most importantly, to whom it sells, you will become more capable of selling more. You not only will be the company that gets those snow blowers or air conditioning units to the people who need them the week before they need them, but you will be the company that is always on, and is always connected.

A great experience is always a great experience. What if you and your spouse were out to dinner on a very special, well-deserved date night, and a week later, you received a thank you note from your server? My

4 Forrester Research 2013

wife and I had this experience, and we frequent that restaurant and recommend it again and again. What if the company that sells the HVAC filters you use in your home ventilation system sent you a reminder email complete with a link to purchase the exact filter when you needed it? Such a company exists, and it makes my life much easier. Individuals and companies that go the extra mile interact and conduct transactions every second of the day and night.

If your company is still (somehow) functioning in an outdated mode and you know success today demands a fast start right out of the gate—don't despair. In this short book you have in your hands, online marketing is about to get even more radical than it already is—you are about to see your customers as you have never seen them before. The fact is, all the old excuses are now ancient: easy-to-use solutions to all your modern-day marketing challenges exist, and as you dig into these pages, you will begin to wonder how your business has survived this long without them.

CHAPTER 2

Connecting With Today's Empowered Customer

When you walk into an auto dealership nowadays, the game is already over—you know it, and so does the salesperson. You know the car and features you want. You know what other people are paying for it—you've been online and done your research. Because they can no longer play the negotiation game like they used to, it is up to the auto dealer to evolve—to connect with you and make service more a part of selling you a car. If they don't evolve, though the specifics may differ, they risk going the way of other brick-and-mortar businesses.

Businesses risk failure nowadays, as we have already mentioned, due to consumers' control of social media. But businesses have to remember too that consumers have considerably more options than they have ever had before. Brand loyalty is no longer a given—it is something a business has to earn, build, and maintain like never before. We can see instances of failure to maintain brand loyalty most clearly with a few brick-and-mortar examples.

Consider Blockbuster's failure and Netflix's success. At the most fundamental level, Netflix listened to complaints customers had with Blockbuster—its lack of selection and late fees—and they swept in, technologically armed, and eventually shut Blockbuster down. Yes, you might be nostalgic for browsing that wall of DVDs and grabbing an oversized box of Whoppers on the way out, but stop there—remember Friday night checkout lines? Your children already have no concept of what it means to wait to see the movie they want to see. And Netflix knows it cannot rest on its laurels—before launching its popular miniseries *House of Cards*, Netflix tested millions of customer preferences.[5] Television—though it may sometimes seem to be just one hundred more channels of garbage—isn't so random anymore. And Netflix no longer stands alone either, with competitors such as Hulu, Amazon, and Google aiming to move above and beyond—to give viewers more of exactly what will keep them glued.

Music is another industry where we can track the

5 Forrester Research.

light speed of changes in terms of an explosion of choice. If your children don't know what a CD is, what would they make of an album? When I was a music fan—and I was a bigger music fan than most—the only source I had for discovering new tunes was my local record store. Even living in a region where I had access to some of the best college non-mainstream radio stations in the country, I relied heavily on my record shop staff to say, "Hey, have you heard of these guys before? They're from Dublin." This shop's staff knew me, they knew what I liked and what I might like, and they offered it to me.

In my college years, there were months I'd walk out of a record store with ten albums or CDs in my bag. That habit stuck with me through my CDNow days as well. Fast forward to 2014, there are very few record stores; instead, iTunes, Spotify, or Pandora give me a hundred choices and recommendations a day. I haven't bought a full album or CD in ages. And though we tend to skip over that odd era for the music industry between the record store and iTunes Genius—the era of Napster when bandwidth was slow and music's legal industry was catching up to the reality of the Internet—that era too significantly broadened music fans' choices.

Of course, not all brick-and-mortar stores need to panic. Not all are headed the way of Blockbuster or

Tower Records—many are adapting. For a while, several big name showroom businesses were hurting as they watched customers come into their stores to literally touch products, only to leave and make an online purchase via Amazon. One of the advantages Amazon originally had over brick-and-mortar stores was its ratings and reviews feature. But now, the always-connected customer realizes he or she can get the best of both worlds. When I recently went shopping for a phone, I went into a local Best Buy with my cell phone in hand. Faced with dozens of options in my price range, I simply pulled out my cell phone, used the RedLaser app to scan my top picks, and then read reviews online. Access to this information was immediate, I used all resources, and I walked out of the store with the phone I wanted.

This kind of mobility-enhanced customer experience is becoming so common we don't even notice it half the time. My cell phone's Passport feature flashes my Starbucks card every time I'm close to a Starbucks—and it tells me how many more lattes I can afford.

As people become more comfortable with—and even unaware of—how much information they share publically, the expectation that companies will take advantage of this information to offer more satisfying and relevant consumer experiences is skyrocketing. How often have you searched online for that perfect winter coat—and found it—only to discover they are sold out in your size? The online shopper who cannot narrow his or her product search on your site by size—or who can't assume you already know his or her size—remember, is very likely to switch to a competitor. Similarly, if you've got the technology in place to suggest related products to your customer, but can't assure availability, you've got an annoyed customer on your hands—why did you even bother? Consumer tolerance for "almost buying the perfect [your product name here]" has been significantly reduced.

We talked in the first chapter about the power and rapidity of a tweet—of all social media—to sound the alarm or sing your company's praises. Gartner research tells us that 97 percent of consumers report that "an online experience influences whether or not they purchase a product" and 89 percent have switched to a competitor "after a negative customer experience." Forrester research calls consumers "digitally armed," and insists that presenting good products and services is only the starting point when it comes to running a successful business these days. What can your company do to ensure you make it out of the starting blocks quickly, and straight into the empowered arms of consumers?

Again, good products and services are only the starting points, and all the technology in the world won't ensure your customers' ability to engage with you in a meaningful and useful manner. Forrester Research points out that of the top three external forces impacting a company, technology rose to first place in 2012, and is unlikely to leave that position in the foreseeable future. Having worked in the online marketing industry since its inception, I have watched companies struggle to patch together solutions across clunky platforms or to grab onto the latest feature sensationalized at a conference (i.e. the ubiquitous the-moment-you-log-in "I'm Cindy, may I help you?" feature). I still see companies taking the strategy-driven annual approach to tech investments. I don't see enough experimentation and risk-taking.

Businesses that look upon mobility and technology as a mere toy will lose the game—some already have. Businesses that are paralyzed by a fear of producing an overwhelming *Minority Report*-type experience for their customers have yet to discover how non-cumbersome new technology can be. We like to think of mobility as being, as Forrester Research has termed it, "the face of engagement." At Monetate, we tell our clients, "When a customer is on your website, you are together, in real time—interact." Customers want fair prices, lasting quality, special features, stellar service, and high performance, whether they are standing in front of you and a pegboard wall of Breedlove guitars, or are browsing the Breedlove website on your phone at 2:00 a.m. while taking the tour bus to their next gig.

Nimble
Emphasizing speed over strength

Flexible
Valuing versatility over lock-in

Global
Embracing worldwide supplies, demands, and markets

Smart
Providing information-rich services rather than dumb products or transactions

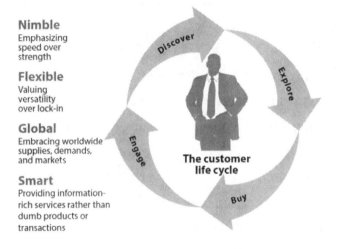

Source: Forrester Research

The empowered customer, aka the digitally armed consumer, expects consistency and responsiveness throughout his or her life. These consumers are spurring competition, and in order to stay competitive, companies must innovate. At the start of the twentieth century, companies like Ford, GE, and RCA ruled what Forrester Research calls the Age of Manufacturing. From 1960–90, we were in the Age of Distribution, with companies such as Walmart and UPS at the forefront. From 1990–2000 in the Age of Information, Amazon and Google broke new ground. From 2010 onward, we live in the Age of the Consumer, in which "empowered buyers are demanding a new level of customer obsession."

While some argue it is a sad sight—throngs of people with their heads down staring into mobile devices rather than engaging in real-life conversations—it is no longer startling. Online conversations are, now more than ever, just another branch of real-life conversing. Customers expect businesses to obsess over them, perhaps because we, as customers, are obsessed. Customers want to build relationships with us as much as we want to build relationships with them—and the bonus? Loyalty is as hip as ever. Customers have access to our company values as much as we have access to theirs. Transparency is almost too simple a word to use when it comes to today's business and consumer relations—indeed, we have moved beyond a form of mutual intimacy to what Forrester Research calls "actionable knowledge."

When we want to renovate one room in our house—say the kitchen—Houzz presents us with over 2 million images. You want ideas for turning your guest room into a home office? Guess how many tutorial videos on putting up a pair of built-in bookshelves you can find. If your CEO is pro-this or anti-that, a certain segment will act upon that knowledge and either bond with you or boycott you. If you discover a certain segment of your customer base is behaving abnormally, you've got tools to take action. We are all online, digitally armed, accessible, or researchable all the time.

Can You Recall The Last Time Your Phone Was *Not* Within Earshot?

63% of smartphone owners keep their phone with them for all but an hour of their waking day. **79%** keep it with them for all but two hours of their day. **1 out of 4** of all respondents didn't recall a time in their day when their phone was not within reach or in the same room.

Whether it is a weekday or weekend, the amount of time away from one's phone didn't vary—it is a *critical tool* for connecting with friends, family and colleagues *every day*.

17%	9%	19%	23%	24%	25%
3 hours or more	2-3 hours	1-2 hours	30 minutes to 1 hour	Less than 30 minutes throughout the day	Never that I can recall was it not close to me

Source: Buffer, July 2013

The data on tablets is likely similar, and growing. As tablets and phones are set to merge into "phablets," obsessing over your customers will grow even more critical. Realizing Pinterest is not just a pretty place to spend one's free time will be crucial.

Staying on top of your field of knowledge or deepening your level of specialization will allow you to thrive in this era where consumers can buy anything they want from a variety of online retailers. For example, Patagonia customers know that Amazon sells tents, fleece, Gore-Tex, and crampons cheaper, but they also know Patagonia's employees are people just like them—outdoors experts and enthusiasts who have tried and tested Patagonia products in a variety of conditions. The company knows that technology is as valuable a tool to survival as its heartiest down parka. Patagonia relies on Monetate tools to optimize experiences across a wide range of niches and regions—serving customers in fifty countries. Patagonia strives above all for authenticity in the sport culture, and says of its partnership with Monetate:

Monetate has really helped us to know our customers better online . . . to create a more fully-featured and fleshed out view of who it is we're speaking to, which allows us to speak to them in a more authentic way . . . Our IT department loves Monetate . . . They're able to test things, try things, and be more experimental with the website. You can get a culture within the company of challenging your assumptions. It's actually really empowering.

Patagonia is just one prime example of how engaging with your customers in a meaningful way produces a win-win situation time and time again, which in turn will translate into more triumphs.

Q7. **Because of social media, I am more likely to:**

80%	Try new things based on friends' suggestions
74%	Encourage my friends to try new products
72%	Stay more engaged with the brands I like
42%	Share any negative experiences with brands or products
32%	Not buy certain products because I learned of a negative customer experience

Just as word of mouth has taken on a whole new level of meaning in today's online world, so too have the elements that comprise a negative customer experience—and will drive 89 percent of consumers straight into the arms of your competition. We have already touched on worst-case scenarios, such as a glitch in the checkout stage, and we have discussed lesser annoyances, such as finding an item you want has sold out. You can sign up for notification of when it comes back in, but aren't told that it will, for sure, be restocked. Think of how businesses that take the simple step of adding the PayPal option to the checkout process win customers.

Think about that time last week when, before turning out the lights, you reached to your bedside table and grabbed your tablet. Lying there in your pajamas, you caught up on some news, watched a *Saturday Night Live* clip for a good chuckle, and then checked in on your favorite sporting goods website—just the sight of some new gear hanging in your closet is going to motivate you this year. You entered the site, searched "running shoes," and added two pairs to your cart, only to discover at the time of checkout that the site doesn't offer PayPal. The last thing you want to do is turn the light back on, get out of bed, walk out of your bedroom, find your wallet, and type in all your information. You abandon your cart and go to a site that takes PayPal and toss in two pairs of socks to go along with your new shoes. Or alternatively, you are at the office sitting right next to the lucky colleague you are in charge of buying a birthday gift for, and you don't want them to know you are shopping. PayPal once again saves the day by allowing you to discreetly make that purchase.

Monetate will give you the tools you need to develop a high-resolution perpetual snapshot of your customers, and these tools will be surprisingly easy to use. We want nothing—especially not time—to get in the way of you getting to know who your customers are, what they want, and when they want it.

CHAPTER 3

What Being Customer-Centric
Really Means

So far this book has made three things clear:

1. Today's customers are smarter and more demanding than ever.

2. Time and timing have never been more of the essence.

3. You have never had a greater capacity and ability to know your customers.

This *Huffington Post* cartoon on the following page is forgetting location, weather, and what time this romantic mutt is getting walked to the park—but you get the picture. Non-canine customers increasingly

"It's the Internet, of course they know you're a dog.
They also know your favourite chew toy, pet food, how
many times a day you go for a walk, and the name of
the poodle at the park you keep sending roses to."

expect your business to provide relevant information
and the products they need and want across multiple
digital marketing channels. Just over one-third of customers expect you to know where they are and what
they are doing, and given the rate at which society is
adapting to the continuous sharing of information, this
number is likely to go up. At the same time, the number of seconds in which you are expected to respond
to your customers' needs and behaviors, is likely to go
down—currently, almost half the customers surveyed

said that they expect response time in any given online experience to take no longer than a minute or two.[6]

A great reputation for customer service is no longer enough. Brands still stuck in the "our customers do this and our customers are that" mentality are standing on quicksand. Nordstrom and Zappos are names we all know and revere; they have each built a strong and loyal customer following. But they also know the time to take the tried and true customer service approach to the next level is now—any business that wants to remain in the game is embracing a customer-centric approach.

In a nutshell: Going customer centric means taking existing customers, and sorting them out into high-value and non-focal customers.

The first step toward becoming a more profitable and successful business is to stop referring to your customers as a single consciousness. "Our customer" does not exist, and it is important that you not just eliminate the term from your vocabulary, but the concept from your mind. You have the possibility to understand now what is unique about each and every one of your customers, and technology is on your side. Remember website changes that used to take months to implement, test, and take down are all a nightmare of the

6 Econsultancy in association with Monetate, "Real-Time Marketing Report," February 2014

past. Today, harnessing the details about what each unique customer is doing on your website takes only a few keystrokes. Imagine how your business could run if your marketing team were armed with the best data gathering and analysis tools. Monetate has these tools.

Monetate did not invent the customer-centric concept. Wharton Business School professor, Dr. Peter Fader, didn't either—but he has done a great job of spreading the customer-centric philosophy and opening eyes to the new marketing mindset. Graduates of today's marketing programs are thinking in terms of gaining the competitive edge by building relationship expertise with each and every customer. Profit is still the goal—it always has been and always will be—but customer centricity proposes a new way of getting there. This new way involves looking at customer behavior above all else, even above what has traditionally been the holy grail of marketing—demographics. The customer-centric business looks at which ad brought which customers to its website, what product they first bought, which referral and channel they came through, and so on. Only after data on behavior is collected, does the most radical step of the customer-centric approach begin.

Dr. Fader notes in his lectures that many businesses resist taking a fully customer-centric approach because it feels risky, or at the very least, challenging. Stating outright what many companies would like to ignore—even if it stands in the way of greater success—requires bravery and energy at multiple levels in a company's hierarchy. Remember a customer-centric approach involves taking existing customers, and sorting them out into high-value and non-focal customers.

In some companies, this kind of move could be deemed unethical—you want us to choose to focus on some customers and not on others? But because this selection is not based solely on demographics—it is not determined solely by socioeconomic factors alone, for example—it is not unethical. It is merely the new way of doing better business, and it is here today and here to stay because technology has made it possible. As Dr. Fader points out, when Henry Ford got his data—he had just sold his millionth car—he didn't know if he had sold one car to a million people or a million cars to one person.

Data allows your company to quickly and easily pick and choose which customers deserve most of your attention, most of the time. The customer is always right and the customer is your focus—these adages still hold true—but we believe they should be even truer for your best customers. We believe, for example, that your best, most loyal customers should never have to wade through steps they have already taken. If you have a million customers, you cannot—and you should not—give the maximum amount of attention to each and every one of them.

This is not to say that non-focal customers should receive mediocre care or treatment—they'll never return if they do. No company goes unscathed in this era of social media if they are found guilty of ignoring even just one customer. The non-focal customer will never have any idea he or she has been put in that segment, but your company will. Your company, when it embraces a customer-centric approach and utilizes all available tools and data in order to do so, will simply reduce spending on the non-focal segment and increase spending and efforts on the high-value segment.

Monetate's predictive analytics tool allows you to look at all traffic on your website, and then go in and measure how well different campaigns are changing— or not changing—customer behavior. In no time at all, you will be able to determine who your most valuable customers are and where they are coming from, so that in turn, you can ensure your company is making the right kinds of investments. You'll see that it is not always the affluence of your customers that affects your bottom line, but sometimes, just what makes sense. Your product might not sell in a well-to-do urban area as well as you thought it would, simply because customers have more access to a wide range of similar products on their way to the office. You might find a rural segment of less wealthy customers is eating your products up, simply because the drive to the closest mall or big name store is a long one.

In the early days of Monetate, we focused on helping our clients target customer segments and take action. But it quickly became clear to us that the data we were collecting was invaluable, and would be an invaluable tool for our clients in terms of taking an understanding of their customers to a deeper level. If one of our clients has determined that affluent married couples are their best customers, that is useful data. However, if this client can then gather additional data tidbits, such as how this couple tends to view and purchase gender-companion products, the value of this data has just increased, and this translates into a better experience for the couple shopping. To put it another way, college students browsing this very same company's website are less likely to view companion products—thus, their experience should be very different. And it can and will be.

Customer-centric marketing does not entail rocket

science, but it does mean that if your company has the customer data, the onus is on you to take advantage of it. Can your customers navigate from the men's puffy jacket to the women's puffy jacket on their own? Of course. But if your company makes the find as convenient and seamless as possible, you have won customers for life.

Humans are not robotically reacting to pieces of data—they are experiencing your efforts and investments in online marketing as a whole. If they have abandoned a shopping cart or have had trouble checking out, you can send them an email either reminding them about that great item they found, offer free shipping, or you can give them a discount if they come back and make the purchase. Today's marketing requires this level of customer development, customer acquisition, and customer retention, no doubt, but it also requires making sure you have the ability to go after and keep the right customers. Data and technology combined, put the power of knowing who is likely to have a higher lifetime value at your fingertips—so that you aren't offering free shipping to 10,000 customers who are spending only five dollars.

Sometimes you do need to make the tough decisions in order to stay competitive. Convincing your company to adapt a customer-centric approach means convincing them that not every customer is worth going the extra mile for. What about the customers that always buy the entire outfit—from socks or sandals right up to the turtleneck or straw hat? What about the travelers who never fail to book a hotel and car with their airline tickets? If your data shows Mr. X always chooses a hotel based on customer reviews and distance to the football stadium, why ask him to request those preferences each and every time? Why not try frontloading his online experience with the services and products he has sought the past nine times out of ten—tossing in just a few impulse items in the sidelines for good measure?

In the past, businesses could legitimately claim it was just too challenging to pull all the data together and to make sense of it. Those claims hold no more. A few trailblazing companies, big and small, have embraced the customer-centric approach, and customers have not only flocked to these businesses, but they now understand what is possible. Today's customer may get frustrated after five clicks instead of ten.

In the mid-to-late nineties, when Internet advertising was first exploding, the idea was to get as many eyeballs on your company's banner in order to drive traffic to your website. The problem was thousands of companies were spending millions of dollars just to garner a lot of traffic, but they couldn't convert the traffic to revenue. Simply put—these companies were overpaying for traffic, in a similar way to how some companies are overpaying now for lesser value or non-focal segments.

We know now that a customer's experience does not start and end with an advertisement or on a website. We can get a sense now of what motivated a customer to come to us in the first place. We can assess their intent in order to make their experience as relevant and meaningful as possible. When a customer leaves our website, chances are we have their email. With the tools we have now, we learn more about each customer each time he or she returns to us. Moving forward with a customer-centric approach means that our most loyal customers receive the lion's share of our resources, our rookie customers receive good care, and because we make each experience relevant and seamless, none is the wiser—all are loyal and content.

CHAPTER 4

Cutting Edge Segmentation Tools and Actionable Data—Moving Beyond the One Collective Customer Mentality

Just as most marketers accepted a 2-percent conversion rate as the norm for so long, most also accepted the notion that optimization tests often did not yield results. Optimization tests on the surface often did not show significant results or would often show significant negative results—and it was the impact at the next level down that was actually most interesting. Tests in the past were run on a mass audience instead of being targeted. Thus tech teams and marketers were much less capable of learning how specific segments were reacting, or not reacting, in response. When impact could not be seen or measured, motivation to make changes or try new things remained—understandably—stagnant.

Today's optimization tools are created with the idea there is no perfect singular website for all, and with targets in mind. These tools are thus able to offer a much more complex and complete picture because they have the power to break down how a particular test affects East versus West Coast customers, or rural versus suburban. "Oh look," a marketing team says, "This test had no impact on affluent frequent buyers, but had a huge impact on customers who abandon their cart more than 75 percent of the time." With results as detailed as these, marketers are able to truly listen to their customers, ask "What's different here?", and try new approaches toward outliers in any direction. Once the basic data parameters are sound, marketers can use what they find in the deeper levels of data and layer them in to change the display for a particular customer based on what is known about him or her at a specific time.

No doubt, in the olden days of online marketing, circa 2000, the data you got out was only as good as the data you put in. Plus, there were limits—data needed to be formatted and compartmentalized because computing power was limited to the number of machines in your data center. Computing power today is an order of greater magnitude, so making sense out of unstructured data is not only possible, but possible on a scale unimaginable a decade ago. Now, with our ever-growing cloud technologies, we know that all the big data we could ever need to improve our business is accessible. The sky's the limit. Big data is the holy grail, the mother ship, the genie in a bottle. "Oh, big data, we have a million customers and we want to know them all!" But of course, the top data challenge reported by retailers is this: We've got too much data.

Most tellingly, when Monetate recruited people for its 2014 annual summit, the top-requested breakout session was Segment Discovery. Specifically, businesses were stating that they had enough data, but they needed our help in finding what data was interesting.

As I have emphasized throughout this book, businesses are interested in who their customers are, now more than ever—mostly, due to social media and increased competition from newer and more innovative companies that were born rejecting the one-size fits-all product-centric marketing model. Companies with CEOs born in the same decade as online marketing are forcing established brands to step up to the plate. No successful business can claim anymore that "We know what our customer wants" because there is no one customer. There is data, and the data shows very distinct and different groups of people who comprise your customer base. You have to not only understand who they are, but what they are doing. If one segment seems lost or different, it is your job to figure out why, and go get them. But even knowing all this, still one-third of businesses report that their marketing team lacks the skills and training to use data to deliver relevant online customer experiences.

So yes, you have the data. You have the technology. You have a team assembled to look at the data and work its magic on the data, but still, you fear that with all this data, you will miss what matters. Paralysis sets in— weren't the old days when technology was less robust and less complicated just simpler? In addition to a lack of skills in translating data to better customer experiences, almost one-third of the companies out there are managing with little or no data at all. Who has time for all this? Monetate, don't you know that of the ten campaigns we try, only two will show anything interesting. We have 1 million customers to attend to—Monetate, are you crazy?

We aren't crazy, and we understand the hesitation regarding big data. We work with this stuff daily and it still blows our mind to think that 90 percent of the world's data has been created in the past two years. We once worked with data in the old-fashioned way too. We recall the data analysts churning it out by hand in the basement, and we recall the heavy reports they threw onto the table as our marketing meetings were about to start—marketing meetings they didn't even stick around for. We know that even now, with all the data we are amassing, at times it still seems you try ten different campaigns and only two show any impact. But we also know this: you have to start down the path of knowing your customers better, and Monetate can help in ways that we, at first, didn't even know we could.

Monetate's predictive analytics tool allows your business to look at data site wide, and then to take it down to various levels. Using our tools, you will work your data at an aggregate level and at a campaign-testing level—and you will work that data quickly without the need for an entire data team. The data being fed into systems now includes social-media data and that of various web and mobile-device experiences, and it is all that much more transparent—with the capability to be used in real time. As I have said before, technology has caught up finally to marketers' dreams. That is not to say IT teams were ever slacking—of course they weren't. But traditionally, their motivation was reporting the data, while the marketers' motivation was reporting the dollar. This disconnect between teams was part of what led to slow change, but thankfully is a thing of the past. Now when you see a sudden surge in interest or in sales—or both—on your website with Monetate you'll be able to narrow down what campaign worked, what aspects of the campaign worked best, and for which customers.

Monetate will allow you to try a dozen campaigns, quickly get feedback on which ones work, and refine and run with those. Even in the case where nothing happens, you will have acquired clues that will enable you to move further along the path toward knowing your customers.

Traditionally, when a marketing team stumbled across a campaign that had a huge impact—it was exactly that, a sort of instance of luckily stumbling across something that hooked customers. But all too often, even if the team could determine what worked, they had no clue why it had. Perhaps the lead marketer would invent a hypothesis and they would continue to push forward with this same campaign for months or years. Labeling a campaign a success and then setting it on a shelf while you ride that success out is not as sustainable as it once was. Embrace the fast-paced-always-connected-world in a philosophical manner or not, but either way, your business must. Is it harder to figure out what your customers need at what time, and what you can provide them in the moment? Yes, it is harder. But this does not mean you have to provide 1 million separate and unique experiences to your 1 million separate and unique customers every second of the day.

The point is to forget the past, not fret about that futuristic future, and to start doing things now with data that you can handle. Remember that you are not obligated to use all of your data, but you do need to fully understand and work off of what is interesting about your data. As technological as it all sounds, the important thing to keep in mind is that your business is about people. If you are a smart marketer, go to your customer service team and ask them what people are complaining about. Never lose sight of the balance between the real-world feedback and data.

Too many companies are struck paralyzed by big data and these companies will fall. Other companies rely on tested but tired methods of throwing one little thing on the campaign fire and assuming that because all is well, that little thing must have done the trick— when in fact, a careful analysis of data would show it did nothing. What's the point? If your company is doing a zillion little things that add up to high-level impact, you are ahead of the guys who are doing two huge things that add up to nothing. If your company is pulling those data people out of the basement and treating them like rock stars—you are on the path to enlightenment and better customer relations, believe it or not.

A truly customer-centric company pushes for its data analysis team to work more closely with its marketing team, and this push is especially relevant in light of the fact that in a recent Columbia Business School study, over half the marketers polled said a lack of sharing customer data within their own organization was a barrier to measuring ROI.

Maybe it is true that in the past, the people we relied on to extract data were not always the most people-oriented employees. They were brilliant at what they did, but they were not charged with driving the business. If they were tasked with creating ten solutions and nine of those solutions were tested and failed, they had done their job in offering up ten solutions. Marketers took the hit, but because there was no mutual incentive—or time set aside—to discover opportunities in the data, opportunities were lost. Money was lost. Customers were lost. Nobody knows how many businesses died, but we know one reason why they might have: because despite having the resources to collect data and review data, nobody could optimize it and turn it into actionable data.

Monetate exists, in part, because of the mistakes we have seen all online marketers make. In the nineties when it all truly began, a business had to run its own servers and build its own platform, which could cost exorbitant amounts of money. Later, as certain platforms became outdated or didn't evolve, re-platforming became popular. Businesses thought the solution to all their problems was to re-platform, when in reality, considerable time and resources were invested, but most of the same problems remained. In essence, many companies still could not get beyond their aggregate data to understand deeper levels of data. Ultimately, re-platforming did not always lead to better customer experiences.

Our predictive analytics tool will allow you to start with a large pool of customers, and to move one level deeper so that you can start making a difference immediately. What are people doing and what are they buying? Is everyone in this particular group doing the same thing, or is there a branch of one group that is acting differently? How nice that you can now spend some time making changes at just one or two levels— targeting that different subset of one segment—and provide more information, give a better explanation, shoot a follow-up email—whatever the data indicates is required. For example, someone is searching your home finance site and they indicate they are looking to refinance or buy a new home. The data tells you their zip code and that you want to retain and talk to these people. On their next visit to your site, they will not have to go three layers deep to find what they are looking for like they did in the old days with the old platforms and old way of IT teams having to jump all the red tape hurdles. You'll perhaps offer a limited time no-fee offer, and you will win that business.

Big data, cutting-edge technology—it's not all about novelty or gimmicks or making sure your website loads within a fraction of a second. The real progression with data and microprocessors and clouds and hives for your customers has to do with everything that happens in the background. If you look at all your big data, most of it is useless—it tells you nothing and it doesn't help you do anything. But when you do find that one thing that helps you change customer behavior, you have to know how to leverage it.

I came to Monetate because I wanted to be part of a team that practiced looking at questions and problems from as wide a variety of angles as possible. I saw that the team at Monetate valued digging deeper in order to reveal what might, in other companies, remain unseen. Companies that work well together, also play well together and their greatest aha moments come not from data, numbers, or profits, but in imagining who their customers are. Talk about your clients—imagine walking them through every aspect of your website on various devices—put yourselves in a thousand customers' shoes. If I were this person looking for that item on such-and-such a device, what might I need or want or expect? What is missing right now? What works for me? Then, check out your team's revelations and insights against some data.

Mastering big data can be done, especially if you keep in mind that the big in big data is really more about the explosion and addiction to social media and mobile devices than it is about some terrifying avalanche of facts and numbers. Big data will not overwhelm or crush you if you set up a few basic rules in managing it.

- Collect and compile data from all sources—from social networks and blogs to your direct mail campaigns.
- Don't be afraid to wed your data analysts to your marketers—or at the very least, to assign a data liaison to translate charts and graphs into meaningful messages for marketers.
- Share and discuss insights across

departments so you can connect the dots and fill in gaps—the angle someone might throw into the mix from sales, or that new intern who has never stepped a foot in a brick-and-mortar store might throw out the flash of genius you've wanted to hear all quarter.

- Set a goal to can stale data, but also to go into each data session with goals so that you don't waste hours digging randomly.
- Don't worry if a few campaigns don't work—these days you have the power to rebound quickly and you'll have ideas for where to go next.

When you use your time, resources, and creative powers, you can make a better customer experience for anyone you can identify as valuable and unique. Data is exploding, but thankfully Monetate has created the tools to harness, tame, and understand it. With these tools in your hands, you can get to the business of your business—producing satisfied loyal customers.

CHAPTER 5

Personalization: It's Much More Than "Hi, Fred."

Some folks think they have created a personalized website with the "Hi, Fred" or "Welcome back, Fred" message, or by offering product recommendations. But in this day and age, just doing the above is only taking a first step down the path of creating a more personalized customer experience. Of course, you can probably guess that in this chapter I am going to tell you what technology exists that will allow you to go much deeper in terms of personalization. If you are offering up the same product recommendations, for example, to existing customers and to new customers, you can do better. If you are offering product recommendations based on what other customers in the same geographic area are looking at, that's a start, but it still is not necessarily as deep as you could or should go.

Monetate makes it easier for you to be smarter about what products you put in front of your customers. Each and every time a customer comes to your site, you will know what kind of device they are using and will be able to seamlessly provide a visually pleasing and easy-to-use customer experience. Your customers—whether they are new to your site or repeat customers—will know without a doubt that they have come to the right place and that they will find what they are looking for. With the right tools working for you, you will be able to determine too, which of your customers holds the highest value for you and should therefore be prioritized.

Over 90 percent of marketers believe that it is important to deliver a winning customer experience, but less than 5 percent believe they are doing so. Part of the problem extends from the fact that for too long, there has been no standard definition of what Customer Experience Optimization (CXO) is and what its goal should be. Monetate begins by defining a working CXO model as one that comprises relevancy, value, authenticity, and timeliness. The goal of CXO is to deliver experiences that enable your customers to win.

Relevancy covers several of the elements we have brought up in previous chapters: Is your site helping a customer who is new to your site to quickly discover what differentiates your business from the hundreds or dozens of other businesses that are similar? Do customers find the best and biggest selection on your site? Is satisfaction guaranteed? A new customer needs to understand the value of your website: why should he or she buy from you? Showing this customer your most popular products is a good tactic. A returning customer should be greeted with relevant products based on past purchasing and browsing behavior. Also, emphasizing what's new will be more engaging to the returning customer and can also instill the idea that the site consistently gets updated to draw them back on a regular basis.

Value relates to the ability of your site to quickly offer the highest-rated product based on what your customer is looking for. Do you highlight products that have been rated highest by existing customers and so on? Adding content to a site or buying guides can help customers buy the right product instead of buying just any product.

In terms of authenticity, does your site make your customer better off? At checkout, are all the coupons that may be applicable to their purchase available? If you exclude negative product reviews, your site is not authentic. If you claim satisfaction guaranteed, but never deliver on it, it is time to change your ways.

Finally, timeliness entails being able to provide special offers that make sense at the moment your customer is online with you. For example, an airline company will alert the customer that the flight they are interested in is almost booked so they should act now. Similarly, if a product is almost out of stock, let your customers know so that when they come back tomorrow or after payday to buy, they won't be let down. Timely also means, in some cases, holding back: allow your customers to spend some time comparison shopping before popping in with a live chat help window.

Of course, none of the above parts of a winning CXO program can function without first taking into consideration the four-part Customer Experience Pyramid, and none of the higher levels on the pyramid can be reached before the base level—structure—is fully established.

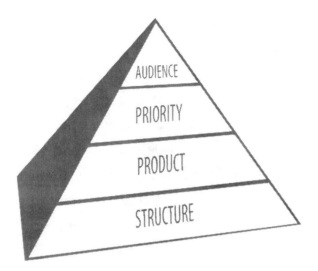

Structure is simply the ability to deliver an optimal customer experience, depending on what device the customer is using to browse your website. Structure is not necessarily simple though—responsive design is not the end all be all of customer experience optimization. Just because the content of your site fits nicely on a variety of screens does not mean it is providing an ideal experience for the end user. If the navigation requires the customer to manipulate or hover over too many option lists, it probably will frustrate a customer on a tablet. If structure is not set up well, tasks such as typing in credit card information to make a purchase can become cumbersome to the point that your customers will drop their shopping carts and take their business elsewhere. Your business must begin with structure, but it must not stop there.

Moving up the Customer Experience Pyramid, product includes product recommendations, but goes beyond just that to include badging and visual site search tools, which help customers wade through a sea of similar products and help them identify what they are looking for through visual cues not just text.

Priority is the third step in the pyramid. This layer depends on all the layers below it, and then adds intelligence to that data in the form of segmentation and business-impact testing. The goal at this stage is to further enhance predictions in regards to segmentation, and to estimate revenue that is generated. Based on what we know about the customer, how should we further refine structure and product? If a customer on a mobile device is close to a store, for example, we will highlight the closest store's information. Business-impact testing measures the effects of a particular CXO technique. For example, we found that by adding a special message for new customers, new customer conversion rates improved by 50 percent. At first glance, if you run a test for a week and only 50 percent of the eligible audience sees the test, the financial impact might appear negligible—a $20K improvement might not seem impressive. However, if every eligible customer receives that new experience just for one month, that $20K could become $160K and that $160K could turn into $1.92M in annualized impact. The key is that in all stages of data review, numbers or statistics that may at first come across as having little impact should be looked at a second time—sometimes, in a different light, you realize you are looking at something huge.

Finally, in the top layer of the pyramid, we have audience. This layer adds to even deeper functions in regards to segmentation. For example, we look at customer loyalty points, browsing behaviors, and so on. This top level looks at data over time, both online and offline with the ultimate goal of delivering a combination of relevant, valuable, authentic, and timely experiences that helps that customer win time and time again.

Just as we caution our clients not to freeze in the face of big data, we explain that it is very important when looking at the Customer Experience Pyramid to recognize the impossibility of scaling it in a single bound. Too many businesses, as we know, are fearful of taking the first step in tackling data. Everyone knows big data is out there and is available as a powerful tool, but all too often they use the big aspect of big data as the very excuse not to embrace it. Even those companies that have taken the plunge often end up doing a whole bunch of ineffectual one-dimensional things with the data—when what the business should be aiming for is a kind of pyramid approach. Many of our clients are utilizing bits and pieces of this pyramid, and are working on filling out the entire picture. Many clients are working hard to acquire the tools that will make their customers' experiences more relevant and rewarding.

Many of our clients have caught wind of what we are doing and are beginning to recognize that technology has evolved to the point of becoming easier to use. Many are also beginning to see that the technologies of just five or ten years ago, which were more expensive, cumbersome, and time-consuming to use are also in this day and age completely ineffectual. In his best-selling book *Microinteractions*, Dan Saffer highlights how discreet functions such as the ease with which a customer is able to log in or provide feedback can make or break his or her perception of a company's service. When the company Starwood changed from offering just a research-and-booking mode to a stay mode when a guest was within forty-eight hours of booking a stay—with maps and directions included, reservations skyrocketed.

The truth is most marketers admit to being surprised at how little they know about what their customers want. Microinteractions make a huge difference for different people in different contexts. Monetate gives you the power to take big data and work on all the little things. If it seems difficult for you to identify whether or not you should get started, know this: You should get started. If it seems challenging to put all the elements of the Customer Experience Pyramid in place, know that it will be a greater challenge to keep up with your competition the longer you wait.

It is not just the big companies that can afford to improve their CXO. Every company of every size can and must find a way into the first layer of the pyramid. Even if you aren't big, think big. List all of the things you want to do regarding CXO, list how big an impact you expect each of those things to make, and then consider the technology required. Sure, bigger companies can work at a more aggressive pace and could put more resources toward this issue, but midsize and smaller companies may have the advantage of fewer old school hurdles and red tape to contend with.

What is your overall business goal? How does your company measure success? What creative resources do you have, and what technological resources do you have?

How can you help bring these forces together? More specifically, how can you optimize customer experiences based on the different visitors coming to your website or via email? When you see you need to make some changes, prioritize these changes based on:

1. Expected return
2. Level of effort involved
3. Buy-in needed before the powers that be sign off

Keep in mind, and remind the key players in your company, that personalization that is based solely on historical data is not deep reaching and powerful enough. Keep in mind the fast-paced multitasking always-connected customer we introduced in the first chapter of this book—the one whose interests and behaviors may change month to month because of what he or she saw on a friend's Pinterest page or read on some movie star's Twitter.

Above all, keep in mind that chances are very high that Monetate has thought all of the obstacles, challenges, and definitions of success through for you— and we can help. Our tools merge the creative and the technological, and our team will show your team how to work marketing magic with the touch of a few buttons. Customer experience optimization is our specialty, and chances are of the twenty-five websites you shop, book travel reservations, or read regularly, we are behind the scenes, helping our clients get to know and serve you better.

CHAPTER 6

What Great Customer Experiences Look Like

Long ago in the early 1990s, when vinyl albums were still common enough and when people had just begun to buy and sell CDs and used CDs, one young music aficionado ventured out into the evening. This young man from Ambler, Pennsylvania, visited several record stores—yes, record stores still existed in abundance back then. On his mission, he would walk directly to the jazz aisle and would stop at the D section. But after doing this several times at several stores, he still could not find what he wanted, which was surprising, because he was looking for one of the most popular albums of all time: Miles Davis's *Kind of Blue.*

Unable to find this famous record in any record store and thinking about how the CD market was swell on the wallet but never truly satisfying—because it was entirely up to chance that a CD you loved and wanted would be in stock the day you happened to be CD shopping—this young man, Jason Olim, saw a huge gap in the music market. From a customer experience standpoint, Olim thought: "Even if a very popular artist has ten platinum records, a store can only carry a certain number of each of them at any given time. I'm going to make all music available to everyone at all times—and then some." This man had no problem getting his twin brother on board with the project.

CDNow launched in 1994, and from its inception, the e-commerce enterprise provided an entirely unique experience for its customers. Marrying rich content to the broadest possible catalog of music enabled music fans to find music they didn't even know they liked or wanted. Music purchasing grew into music discovery, which led to more purchasing. Innovative plans such as Cosmic Credit, which leveraged rabid music fans' own web pages and fan pages as music profiling tools and advertising bases, drove sales in return for store credit. The brothers who created CDNow led a rags-to-riches fairy tale in their time, even beating out former industry giants Tower Records and Blockbuster.

Examples of companies that pushed the limits early on abound. The limits they had to contend with were serious too, but these companies pushed through, and those that survived the dot-com bust and the economic disaster of the mid-2000s did so because they always thought of customer needs first. Good business is never about business first. Yes, we have to always consider the bottom line, but if the customer gets wind the bottom line takes precedence over their whims, needs, and desires—business loses. People who recognize a gap in the customer experience in any realm, and who can act fast to fill that gap, create those businesses that cause others to hit themselves over the head and say, "Now, why didn't I think of that?"

Half.com was another early online innovator. Taking advantage again of a perceived and definite lag in what customers needed and what they were begrudgingly accepting, Half.com founders married customers who wanted to sell their books with an existing book database. It might be worth it to recall that eBay in that era was problematic for booksellers to use because for each book a seller wanted to offer, a description had to be written up. If someone was trying to sell hundreds of books for just a few dollars each, the time spent on cataloguing everything would render the enterprise unprofitable. Half.com's system, on the other hand, was sheer genius: it simply asked the bookseller to enter in the book's ISBN or UPC label and automatically that book would be matched with its title, author, and an already existent description. The system solved problems not only in the selling experience, but in the buying experience as well since a rating and pricing system based on the book's condition—new, excellent, good, fair, poor—was built-in.

Harkening back to those old names—CDNow, Half.com, Tower Records, Blockbuster—thinking back to just a decade ago, before online shopping caused some of the brick-and-mortar stores to shut down, it might be tempting to wax nostalgic. No such thing. Online shopping and always-on customers has forced companies to truly innovate and put the customer first. Brick-and-mortar stores survive now and indeed thrive as never before in combination with their online sites and online marketing efforts. When True Religion jeans decided it needed to drive in-store traffic and awareness about a new product line, it came to Monetate for help. Using our tools to run a dynamic email campaign on a scale they were not able to run before, the luxe jeans company sent out 65,000 geo-targeted email messages, which resulted in a 1 percent in-store conversion rate. While this number may at first appear small, in reality, a significant number of this subset of True Religion customers left their home, drove to a store, and took advantage of the one-time $50 off offer just for trying True Religion on.

The True Religion example shows what can happen when a company that knows its database is lacking in a fundamental but critical way decides to take action. Jeans are a product people particularly need to try on, and once you win a client over and they know how your brand fits, you can rest a bit easier, figuring they will buy online or in-store, in a hybrid fashion, into the future.

Some companies operate in an almost entirely hybrid fashion. Homeclick.com is a perfect example of the hybrid experience. As a company that targets higher middle-class home renovators, they ask visitors to view their products as an industry professional or not. For the DIY-type who wants to purchase $10,000 worth of high-end materials, but will have someone do all the installation, Homeclick.com offers unbeatable online and phone sales support. Customers who would normally have little access to the type, range, and pricing structures of products upscale professional contractors might have, benefit from this partly DIY/partly do-it-for-me hybrid experience.

Despite the notion we may have sometimes, that in this day and age every need we could ever imagine having fulfilled is being fulfilled, there are still plenty of holes in the customer experience. A few years ago and several years into their success, the team at vintage fashion and decor retailer Modcloth asked what sorts of online shopping experiences left them feeling disappointed. The idea of seeing a pair of shoes that would be the perfect match to a dress that had never been worn before—only to discover the shoes were out in your size was noted as a major let down. The best items always do seem to go first, and if you can't be online 24/7 with your credit card in hand, you might miss out. To alleviate some of the pain customers might feel when the item they want is out of stock, Modcloth created a simple form which would allow them to notify a customer via email when a desired but unavailable item came back in stock.

In addition to relieving the itch of having found the item of your dreams, but thinking you might never be able to possess it, Modcloth takes a unique approach to its merchandising, asking customers to vote on new products and designers. Customers not only curate the merchandise, but they are asked to name dresses with whimsical names, and they can opt in to receive special offers and access to unique vintage items. Illustrating the level of customer dedication and engagement is the fact that over fifty percent of Modcloth customers share their body measurements in onsite reviews, doing so in order to indicate which brands tend to run true to size, or overly large or small—and to ultimately help other members of the Modcloth shopping community find exactly what they are looking for. Of course, Modcloth can then leverage this information to reveal brands that are most likely to fit a specific customer's body, that is, where one brand's size 6 is a true 6, another brand's size 6 might fit like a 4. Collecting this data via customer input and via shopping history—including exchanges and returns—helps Modcloth continually refine the content it presents when a visitor logs on. Indeed, many Modcloth customers visit the site more than half a dozen times a day.

Modcloth continues to soar, and while its customers are flying around the globe in their vintage frocks and vintage sunglasses, they might take note of one premier coalition loyalty program Aeroplan. Most of us would be hard pressed to find a friend or colleague who is thoroughly impressed with their airline's mileage and benefits program, but Aeroplan could change the industry's bad reputation. In 2013, with the end goal being to better reward its members, they used Monetate's tools to better target and reach out to customers enrolled in any one of the three tiers in their mileage-rewards plan. When customers were approaching a certain tier, specific content was pushed to them, in order to entice them to achieve that next status level.

Uber is another rock star company that has been expanding since its inception in 2009. Users sign up for Uber, which is essentially a glorified taxi service or a car service that does what taxis cannot do. With your credit card information stored and access at all times to your location, Uber allows you to assure a car will be waiting right outside your door at the exact moment you need one. No more hailing cabs or waiting for the cab dispatcher service to answer your call and put the call out. No need to find a quiet spot in the restaurant or at the party so you can give your name, phone number, and address. Push one button on your phone during the encore of your favorite band's concert, and your phone will begin to count down the minutes remaining until your safe ride home arrives.

Customers whose ride of choice happens to be a motorcycle are probably aware of the innovative customer experience RevZilla provides. Launched in 2011, with an online and offline presence, RevZilla prides itself in offering what no other motorcycle store can.

With over 3,000 in-house video clips on everything from gloves to parts to gear bags, RevZilla leads the pack in thought leadership in their industry. The sales team prides itself not only on being motorcycle experts, but on being enthusiasts—just like their customers. Their business is not just about selling, but about loving the ride, the journey, and the thrill of it all.

Innovation in the online shopping experience is the thrill of it all. We have said it once and we'll say it again: now is the time for marketers to push their ideas forward and to grab on to all available tools to put those ideas to work. It is time for marketers and IT departments to communicate as they never have before. It is time for CEOs to let out some of the rein and encourage people to seek out the holes and gaps that do still exist in the online shopping experience. Find what isn't working smoothly, determine what causes customers to disengage, and talk about what is just sometimes a pain in the neck in your own personal online shopping experiences—and take action. Once you stop thinking primarily about filling your own coffers and approach the way you build your customer experience in terms of what is most appealing, relevant, and valuable to your customers, you will not fail.

CHAPTER 7

How Today's New Technologies Have Changed Everything and What They Can Do for You

If you were asked to close your eyes right now and try to imagine sitting in front of your home computer in 1995, what would that look like? What would you see on the screen in front of you and how long would it take you to see it? Is it even possible to recall how long it took to send and receive an email back then? How many pages did you have to browse through to do your online shopping—wait, did you do any online shopping prior to 2000? Wasn't it just quicker to drive to your local mall?

Commercialization of the Internet—using the Internet as a way to make money rather than just to communicate—began in earnest in the mid-nineties. One of the most significant early challenges in setting up shop online had to do not with products or merchandising or logistics, but with bandwidth—a company not only had to own its own servers, which were very expensive, but these servers had to support regular and holiday traffic as well. This meant that a company might have to throw away significant sums of money during slow sales months just to make sure their site was fully scaled and working smoothly during heavier sales months. If you asked your teenage daughter to revisit one of your favorite pre-twenty-first century online stores, she would laugh, pull at the hair on her head, scratch her chin, probably hit the computer, and look at you as if you were lucky to have survived the Jurassic Period.

In the mid-nineties, the speed at which your online store functioned depended entirely on how fast the pipeline coming into your building worked. During this time period, the earliest online product managers were folks who had come out of the CD-ROM and content design fields. The world of online media and retail in the mid-nineties into about 2000—rested mainly in the hands of operations teams and software engineers. It is hard to remember now, when we use our laptops, tablets, and phones to conduct any number of online purchases daily, that online shopping was once a blank slate—a hyper-rudimentary process. Many companies in those early dot-com days were literally burning through millions of dollars per month. The market was going crazy, young college graduates were making six-figure salaries right out of the gates, and investors could see nothing but green fields of opportunity ahead.

When the dot-com bubble burst though, even the big guys felt the crunch—even Amazon.

Of course, as we all know, after the bubble burst, technologies rebounded and continued to evolve. Online businesses continued to change, grow, and thrive—in a savvier and saner way. The concept of creating unique and relevant experiences for customers began to creep steadily along—with the beginnings of personalization showing in the use of customers' first names in emails. In the mid-nineties, the main key to a company's online success still was couched in terms of driving traffic to its website—the higher the number of eyeballs on your web page, the higher the value (or so it was thought) of your company.

Banner advertising was huge then, and so was a company's cost at promoting and sustaining these ads. With costs ranging from $50–$100 per one thousand impressions to run a banner ad, it is easy to see how companies did burn millions. Factor in the statistic that only 1–2 percent of Internet visitors ever clicked on a banner ad, and you wonder—why and how did online retailers rely on them at all? Sure, you could buy a chunk of banner ads consisting of content that would better target your Yahoo audience and another chunk of ads that would be tailored to your RollingStone.com audience, thus personalizing a potential customer's experience somewhat—but the bottom line was that the only thing marketers could control in the twentieth century was the on-site eyeball count.

Testing was prohibitively expensive too. The number of hours and IT people it took to divert half a website's traffic away for testing was insanely high. We have already discussed in this book the problem with building and maintaining in-house platforms, but again, even once a platform was up, in the mid-nineties it could take up to twelve months to then optimize it.

CDNow was one company that was ahead of the game in terms of how it ushered forth a holistic approach to the online customer experience. By aiming not just for record sales, but to create something meaningful for its customers, CDNow was one of those pioneering companies that believed they were revolutionizing the way business was conducted online—and they were.

And then the early 2000s came, and several of the early e-commerce revolutionaries experienced the double-whammy of their next huge thing naturally dying out and the dot-com bust.

The year 2000 saw the emergence of companies carving up pieces of online operations and structuring business around each piece. Servers were no longer run entirely in-house, and though testing platforms and personalization tools still required IT-centric teams to build and run them, tech muscle and creative potential were beginning to meet up—or to at least be present in each other's sights. Tools were not yet easy for marketers to use, but companies were beginning to see that tools needed to evolve so that marketers could move beyond advertising, promotion, and driving traffic.

Enter Monetate and the Cloud in 2008. Early Monetate tools were amongst the first of their kind, in terms of being—or aiming to be—more marketer-friendly. With our tools, marketers could begin to do what they wanted on the website side of business—they could target specific customers with specific messages, they could put the right item in front of the right customer at the right time, and they could measure the impact of these moves. While still much more technologically focused than business-focused in the early days and still limited by bandwidth, code, and platforms, we always kept our eye on the prize. We knew that when a new customer came to a client's website, we wanted to enable that client to discuss shipping and returns, highlight the company's one-hundred year history, or emphasize staff expertise. Our earliest tools required some IT skills, but we knew we wanted to keep honing those tools so that they seriously empowered marketers.

Marketers now have more freedom to act in the moment anytime and anywhere. Marketing tools such as Paypal Beacon and Nomi are redefining the in-store and online shopping experience—merging the best of both worlds, and indeed, creating new ones. Instead of manually alerting your device that you are in XYZ Café like you had to do with Foursquare, these new tools require you to do nothing but sit back and browse, comparison shop, and purchase. Connecting with a merchant's in-store Wi-Fi signals or with small sensors in the entryway, Nomi tracks a customer's entire visit. How much time does the customer stay in the store and how much time does he or she spend in each department? Nomi can even determine which products a given customer has stopped to inspect—with a one- to three-meter range of accuracy—and provide an on-the-spot deal. Nomi tracks purchases, but it can also determine whether a deal offer resulted in a one-time spike in customer purchases or in the conversion of an entirely new group of regular customers.

Beacons could be called the no-nonsense in-and-out shopper's best friend. PayPal Beacon allows users to walk into a store, find the product they want, and buy it without ever having to talk to a human being. The always-on customer pays and goes.

As with all emergent technologies, there is always an initial creepy feeling. Marketers know you went to this store in this city and walked down only three aisles but spent twenty minutes in that third aisle. Your phone sends you a coupon. You look around the store; a shiver runs down your spine. But you do really need that new printer and you could really use the immediate $10 discount so you go for it. You drive home, imagining some large eye in the sky following you. The eye knows your car's make and model, knows which gas stations you prefer, and knows, perhaps, it is time to change your oil. You get home with your new printer, after having used your extra ten dollars to have your oil changed. You don't bat an eye or realize what went on behind the scenes, and you don't care because you saved money and took care of business.

There is enough technology now that we can declare that the onus of driving new business is entirely on the marketers' shoulders. Nobody is limited by technology now, and nobody can claim big data is too overwhelming. To make an impact, you only need to take a handful of findings you have gleaned from your data and do something compelling with them. Put the idea of people back in to all the ideas of technology and empower your business to attract more people. Customers are always on and are always cognizant of how and when a company is thinking of them. Show your customers that you are ahead of the curve, and they will use that ever-so-mighty device they hold in their hands to spread the word.

CHAPTER 8

Putting It All Together: Creating Your Next Marketing Campaign

These days, it is non-digital executives who are hitting the glass ceiling. Leaders with digital chops are now, more than ever, the ones to watch. Companies that focus on the value of learning about failure and success will succeed. Technology, while seemingly advancing at lightning speed over the past decade in particular, has actually finally caught up to the minds of marketers, which have always been working just one millisecond faster. Not taking advantage today of the meld between the marketer's mind and the tech tools available is foolish. Marketers who are willing to embark on the challenging journey of creating better customer experiences are changing not just the way people conduct their online shopping, but the way people socialize, communicate, and live.

Optimizing customer experience is what we are after. Start at your website's home page—or start at the first page any number of your customers is likely to land—and take a step back and analyze where you are deficient at a universal level. Keep in mind too at this point, your home page is not always the first page seen, so if you have been focusing all your attention there, take two steps back.

When a visitor first enters your site, what device are they coming in on and who are they? What is their first impression? As they begin to explore your products, how do they find what they are looking for—are they browsing, using a product search, or pulling items up by category? Once your customers find what they are looking for, how easy is it for them to make their selection? Do you mention your shipping policy and describe what distinguishes your product from others? When your customer is on your product detail page, is the add-to-cart option located beneath the fold? Is your check out and conversion process optimized for maximum customer ease and satisfaction?

Considerations such as those mentioned above can have a huge impact on your audience. If you run every aspect of your customer's online experience—landing page, exploration, selection, and check out—through the Customer Experience Pyramid—structure, product, priority, and audience—you will be forced to view your website through fresh eyes and start learning what needs to be improved. Phase one then, is about fixing things that would be considered deficient or confusing to anybody coming to your website.

Looking at the same site and considering what needs to be changed to make it more helpful or useful to broad single-dimension audience segments is the second phase of optimizing customer experience. New customers versus returning customers, male versus female, East Coast versus West Coast, and so on—you need to define who is visiting your website. From there, determine what kinds of messages engage each segment most. New customers might like to know what makes your company and products unique; returning customers might appreciate seeing what's new or being able to return to the shopping cart they left behind during their last visit.

Phase three entails adding multiple layers of segmentation to the basic segments you created in the previous phases. Here is where you would apply changes specific to multiple audience attributes—you have a new customer on an iPhone near your physical store. Phase three is the refining phase, and it takes a much deeper look at customer behavior. If a returning female customer from San Francisco has come to your website, here is where you also determine the affluence of her particular zip code, how often she has shopped clearance with you in the past, and perhaps what the most expensive items she puts in her cart are. Does she follow through with her purchases 100 percent of the time, or only 50 percent, and what factors seem to influence or correlate to that difference? In the recent past, attempting to parse out all these various aspects of one in 100,000 customers was next to impossible; today, tools exist to handle it all—you just need to get your hands them.

Moving through the three phases of creating a better customer experience usually does not happen overnight. We at Monetate have engaged with hundreds of companies and we have watched them slowly, sometimes over a period of several years, take on the challenge of experience optimization, and go on to succeed. Companies that visualize themselves moving through Monetate's Customer Experience Pyramid find a solid and reliable methodology with which to tackle what at first might feel radical, risky, or overwhelming.

From that very first landing a customer makes on your web page, earning their time and their purchase requires certain tactics. Knowing a customer entered your website after searching with the keyword "dresses," enables you to present photos of dresses—as opposed to shorts. Helping your customer to then discover more of what she might need or want is the next step. Knowing some basic data about your customer base enables you to create a dozen or more basic entry point personas. From there, what are you doing to help the stay-at-home mom, college athlete or jet-set explorer find what they are looking for? Are you badging dresses in a variety of categories such as new, as seen in Hollywood, or customer favorite? Can your customers quickly and easily read customer reviews, and at an even deeper level, can they read reviews by top-rated customers who are broken down into the same age and body type, as well as view photos of real customers wearing your dresses? If you are selling hotel rooms and you already know your customer prefers only four-star accommodations, are you wasting their time and cluttering their web experience by presenting two-star options?

Make it easy for your customers. Get them to your site lead them through an enjoyable journey of discovery, and then aid them in the selection process. If you can see your customer is close to making a commitment—they have chosen a size and color and have read ten reviews—make sure you are presenting every piece of information that customer needs in order to say, "Yes, this is the right dress/hotel room/membership status for me."

Ultimately, the Customer Experience Pyramid should end in the customer finding what they are looking for. That customer should finally give you their email contact information or make that purchase. You have set and reinforced expectations; you have shown your customer you are ahead of the curve and are genuinely paying attention to their each and every move. As your company moves further along, making a potentially bigger impact upon a larger and yet more specific customer base will be possible. If you begin to notice that your offer for free shipping for purchases over $100 is rarely used—the average of all customer purchases is $89—you can begin to adjust either your offer or your pricing structures, in order to change the behavior of customers moving forward.

Knowing that you do not have to run this better customer experience race in zero to sixty—that in fact, most companies cannot and do not—will empower you to start making the changes that you can make today. Tools exist that allow you to optimize email. In the old days, Jane Doe received a predetermined email from you every thirty days: Dear Jane, Please take advantage of our limited time offer of 20 percent off XYZ. Fast-forward to today and you can send Jane an email offering rain boots when you know she is in Seattle.

The point is no company, large or small, is expected to work through the Customer Experience Pyramid all at once—but you must start somewhere. Most websites do allow customers to do what they want to do—most are not fundamentally flawed, but there is always room for improvement. Marketers today can slice and dice people according to the type of device they are on—meaning they can adjust content and processes accordingly. Marketers today have the ability to measure customer behavior in ways previously unimagined—we now know with precision what customers actually need, want, do, and say.

Measurement drives marketing, and while improving your customer experience will take some time, the time to act aggressively is now. Measuring no longer takes inordinate amounts of time, money, and staff. It no longer needs to slow down your marketing campaigns. Yes, measuring is complicated, but machines will do the work, while humans get started on that first small step of making a first good impression. Over the long term, the more you experiment on your website, the more you will understand who your customers are, and who your best customers are. Do put yourself in your customers' shoes and embrace the idea of experimentation. Do not expect big impact from small changes and do not be afraid of change. Online marketing is moving into its third decade of life—it is time to be bold.

CHAPTER 9

A Gaze Into the Future of the Online Experience

Back in the 1950s, people believed that by 1980, we'd all be driving flying cars through multi-dimensional intersections. Those of us who grew up watching the cartoon *The Jetsons* imagined how convenient some of those five-course meals in pill form might be—tasteless and less romantic perhaps, but at least we would all be eating our vegetables. In the 1990s, when I first got involved in online marketing, I envisioned that surely by 2010 we would all be shopping in fully virtual 3D stores. Of course, none of these futuristic notions has proven entirely true, but what has proven true is the fact that technology has developed faster in the past few years than ever before. Today, the AMC smash hit *Mad Men* reminds us not only how very far we have come in terms of office politics and practices, but how advertisers and marketers have evolved in regard to their customers desires, needs, and expectations. Today's customers—as we have stressed throughout this book—are demanding that marketers step up their game.

An entire generation now exists that has grown up online. It's true that some college students have never used a postage stamp. There is a world of customers out there who share their every want, need, and dream daily online—and marketers are rushing to keep up with the possibilities and opportunities. The futuristic notion of being able to know if a customer you will never meet live is young or old, regular or new, East Coast or West Coast, happy or sad—is now a reality. Today's customers, young and old, do share data—the kind of data marketers have always sought to collect and have collected. But it is only very recently, that marketers have had the technology and the tools to do something meaningful with these vast amounts of data.

In the *Mad Men* era, the customer was seen as naïve, and the tone of many advertising and marketing campaigns was condescending. In their glorious offices from behind their fabulous desks, the men—for the most part—collected data based on their wives' or their secretaries' personal choices and opinions. Once in awhile test groups were invited in to eat doughnuts and discuss a new line of makeup or pantyhose, but in general, data was hard to come by. The customer was considered a heterogeneous group, hence the slogan "We know our customer" was born, and it reigned for decades. Yes, when we watch *Mad Men* and see how much time was spent on perfecting jingles, we smirk, but the bar in advertising and marketing—no pun intended—is now set much higher.

Data is now available as are the tools to do something with it. And because we are moving into an era where everyone is on, all the time, that data will only get more interesting. Today's consumer lives with his or her device in hand, and those devices are evolving. Our phones have gotten smaller and lighter, our tablets are on our bedside tables, and soon we might all be donning a pair of Google glasses or perhaps an amazing high-tech watch. By 2020, brick-and-mortar shops will still exist, but it is highly likely customers will be walking into those stores wearing devices they will use to shop with—and they won't even have to carry their shopping tools in their hands.

Technology has a way of disappearing into the background, and it is only going to become a less distinct part of our daily existence and functioning. When we do stop to think of the huge leap our tools have taken, from the first twenty-pound laptop to today's paper-thin version, we see clearly the change. The difference in visual quality between the old tube TV of the nineties and the DVD then the DVD and high-definition TV is quite impressive—but only when we take a moment to recognize it. Otherwise, most of us absorb technological changes like a sponge. And for younger generations especially, rapid technological change is as taken for granted as the sunrise.

Technology and data collection are fading into the background as they become ever-present factors of our lives. Customers are walking into stores armed with tools that assist them in finding deals and making purchases, and on the other end, smart marketers are using their own tools to better refine their customers' experiences. In the future, marketers will be able to track, collect, and analyze every step of every customer experience. For example, marketers will know if someone has come to their company website through site Y or through site Z, if 50 percent of their customers fit persona A or persona B, and the mood of a particular customer on any particular day. In the future, marketers will be able to provide customers with an experience that nails it before they have even made a purchase.

It was only just a few years ago that the online

marketing and retail experience truly began to change. Netflix had to rely on DVD rentals until bandwidth speeds caught up to the service the company truly wanted to provide—streaming. Running tests on marketing data took high-tech teams and time. Costs were prohibitive. But now there are tools that allow less sophisticated users to do more sophisticated things. Monetate continues to design, test, and build tools that will become easier to use and more powerful—tools that will land in the hands of marketing rock stars who want to create a unique, relevant, and satisfying customer experience for each and every customer. Websites are already becoming more and more personalized, and yet customers sense less and less the technology behind these personalized interactions. These trends will continue.

Remember, there was a time when Google didn't exist. There was a time when not all companies emailed you. Heck, you sometimes didn't check your email for days. There was a time—and sadly for some the hangover still exists—when marketers believed that driving more people to their site meant they were succeeding. For decades, technology was too expensive not only for large corporations to manage, but for consumers to own and use. Now everyone has a laptop, tablet, or a mobile phone. Now is the time marketers must take advantage or risk becoming obsolete like Blockbuster and the shopping mall.

Prototype stores and kiosks that run with no human staff are popping up. You can go to any major US airport and board your flight without talking to another human being if you choose. Technology is getting it right more and more—ask your average consumer on the street what changes he or she has noticed in the past twelve months alone on his or her favorite online sites. Again, some of the changes, customers will notice: the skis they abandoned in their shopping cart will pop up on their Facebook page or a membership they were considering last week but hesitating on suddenly is being offered to them via email at a discount. Some of the changes will never be obvious to customers, but companies who use this as an excuse—"I don't know where to begin to make changes!"—will be left behind.

Driving personalization must be a top priority for all businesses today. Perfecting jingles, driving traffic to your website, and running a one-size-fits-all campaign are marketing techniques of the past—the distant past. If Amazon has already begun using drones and your company is stuck in an early 2000s mindset, it is time to up your game. Remember customers have the ability to share good news, reviews, and leads—and you want all of that goodwill to funnel directly to your business. Even with limited resources, you can commit to prioritizing and to doing something today with the data you have with the help of Monetate.

CPSIA information can be obtained at www.ICGtesting.com
Printed in the USA
BVOW03s1602160415

396472BV00004B/8/P